The President Is a Lot
Smarter Than You Think

Doonesbury books by G. B. Trudeau

Still a Few Bugs in the System
The President Is a Lot Smarter Than You Think
But This War Had Such Promise
Call Me When You Find America
Guilty, Guilty, Guilty!
"What Do We Have for the Witnesses, Johnnie?"
Dare To Be Great, Ms. Caucus
Wouldn't a Gremlin Have Been More Sensible?
"Speaking of Inalienable Rights, Amy . . ."
You're Never Too Old for Nuts and Berries
An Especially Tricky People
As the Kid Goes for Broke
Stalking the Perfect Tan
"Any Grooming Hints for Your Fans, Rollie?"
But the Pension Fund Was Just Sitting There
We're Not Out of the Woods Yet
A Tad Overweight, but Violet Eyes to Die For
And That's My Final Offer!

In Large Format

The Doonesbury Chronicles
Doonesbury's Greatest Hits

a Doonesbury classic by

G.B. Trudeau.

The President Is a Lot Smarter Than You Think

An Owl Book   **Holt, Rinehart and Winston / New York**

To the memory of C.C.

Published by Holt, Rinehart and Winston,
383 Madison Avenue, New York, New York 10017.

Published simultaneously in Canada by Holt, Rinehart
and Winston of Canada, Limited.

Library of Congress Catalog Number: 72-78133

ISBN: 0-03-091406-X

Printed in the United States of America

The cartoons in this book have appeared in newspapers
in the United States and abroad under the auspices of
Universal Press Syndicate.

9   10   8

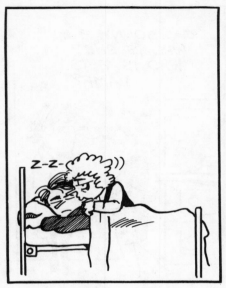

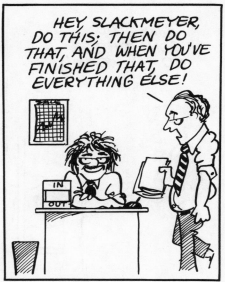

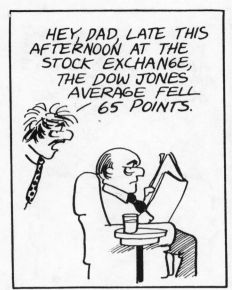

Dear Michael, You'll be happy to hear I am working hard.

This is because I want to go to college after all.

When I do get to college, I'm taking a combined major of English and Urban Studies.

I'm planning to be an enlightened slum-lord.

GB Trudeau

Dear Mr. Attorney-General; I've been meaning to write you a fan letter for some time.

I particularly want to congratulate you on the way you and the D.C. police chief handled those smelly peace freaks last spring!!

I thought it was neat the way you suspended the constitutional rights of those stupid long-hairs and clutched them in jail. What a _delightful_ surprise!

Silly me — I had no idea you were allowed to do that.

G.B. Trudeau

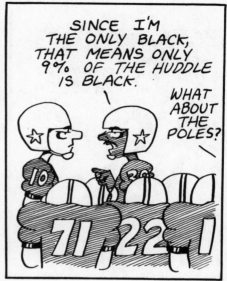

WE INTERRUPT THIS PROGRAM TO BRING YOU A SPECIAL MESSAGE FROM THE WHITE HOUSE...

GOOD EVENING, MY FELLOW AMERICANS. I JUST WANTED TO TELL YOU THAT I HOPED YOU WERE ALL ENJOYING MY 90 DAY FREEZE.

LOWER TAXES, NO PRICE INCREASES— PRETTY GREAT, HUH?.. SO NEXT YEAR, WHEN YOU'RE THINKING ABOUT THE CANDIDATES, LOOK AT MY RECORD, O.K.?.. WILL YOU DO THAT FOR ME?.. FINE!

GBTrudeau

AND NOW BACK TO "THE BEVERLY HILLBILLIES."